HISTORY'S GREATEST DISASTERS

THE FLU PANDEMIC OF 1918

by Kristin Marciniak

Content Consultant
Nancy K. Bristow
Professor of History
University of Puget Sound

CORE
LIBRARY

Published by ABDO Publishing Company, PO Box 398166, Minneapolis, MN 55439. Copyright © 2014 by Abdo Consulting Group, Inc. International copyrights reserved in all countries. No part of this book may be reproduced in any form without written permission from the publisher. The Core Library™ is a trademark and logo of ABDO Publishing Company.

Printed in the United States of America,
North Mankato, Minnesota
042013
092013

♻ THIS BOOK CONTAINS AT LEAST 10% RECYCLED MATERIALS.

Editor: Jenna Gleisner
Series Designer: Becky Daum

Library of Congress Control Number: 2013931971

Cataloging-in-Publication Data
Marciniak, Kristin.
 The flu pandemic of 1918 / Kristin Marciniak.
   p. cm. -- (History's greatest disasters)
ISBN 978-1-61783-956-6 (lib. bdg.)
ISBN 978-1-62403-021-5 (pbk.)
Includes bibliographical references and index.
1. Influenza Epidemic, 1918-1919--Juvenile literature. 2. Epidemics--Juvenile literature.   I. Title.
614.5--dc23

                                        2013931971

Photo Credits: National Museum of Health/AP Images, cover, 1, 10; PhotoQuest/Getty Images, 4; MPI/Getty Images, 7; Library of Congress, 9; Harris & Ewing Collection/Library of Congress, 13; Bettmann/Corbis/AP Images, 14, 21, 25, 31; Getty Images, 18, 33; Hulton Archive/Getty Images, 23, 36; Red Line Editorial, 26, 39; Time & Life Pictures/Getty Images, 28, 45; Toby Talbot/AP Images, 41

CONTENTS

THE FIRST CASE

Something was very wrong in Haskell County, Kansas. It was late February 1918. A mysterious disease was racing through the small farming town. People who had been healthy just a few days earlier now suffered from fever, headaches, aches, and pains. For some people, the disease turned into a violent case of pneumonia. Their lungs filled with fluid, making it difficult for them to breathe.

After the flu began spreading, men at some camps gargled salt water to help protect themselves from the influenza virus.

The Warning

Haskell County doctors were alarmed. The disease seemed like influenza, or the flu, but it was spreading much more quickly and affecting many more people than in years past. One doctor warned public health officials about the disease, but there was little they could do to prevent it from spreading.

Influenza Symptoms

When someone came down with the influenza virus that began in Haskell County, the symptoms usually lasted approximately three days. Victims developed a headache, a high fever, and chills. Their eyes burned, and their muscles ached. Even though there were deaths in the first months of the virus, they were rare.

A Different Kind of Flu

In 1918 it was not necessary for doctors to report an outbreak of influenza. The flu was usually mild. Most people recovered after a few days of rest. Like most diseases, traditional influenza was the most dangerous for very young children and the elderly. But the flu

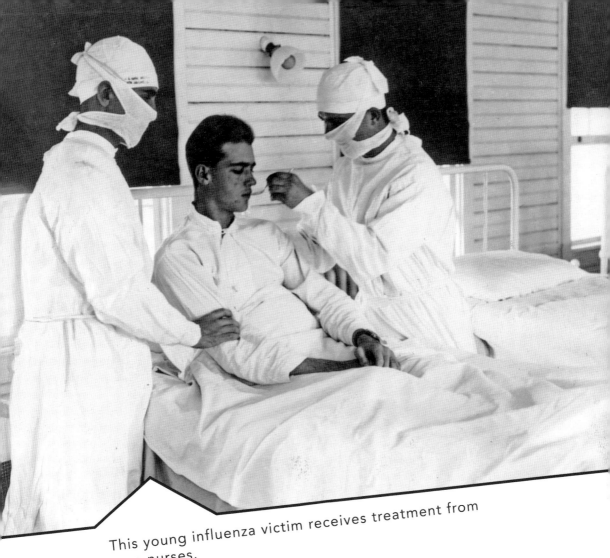

This young influenza victim receives treatment from two nurses.

in Haskell County in the winter of 1918 seemed different. Young adults in their 20s and 30s were hit hardest by the disease. A few even died. Public health officials decided to report the 18 cases of flu to the federal government in March. But it was too late.

Life in the Barracks

Camp Funston was overcrowded, and the winter of 1917–1918 was harsh. Tents were not heated, and the men did not have enough warm clothing. They huddled together in front of stoves to keep warm. All of this close contact made it easy for the disease to spread.

First Wave Begins

At the end of February, a soldier from Camp Funston in Fort Riley, Kansas, came home to Haskell County. He didn't know the town was under attack by a rapidly spreading disease. He returned to Camp Funston a few days later, as did two other Haskell County men. One of them had a sick child at home. All three men arrived at the base between February 28 and March 2, 1918.

On March 11, 1918, a cook at the army base reported to the infirmary with a sore throat, fever, and headache. By noon, 100 more men reported the same symptoms. Within a week, 500 men at the base

Camp Funston in Fort Riley, Kansas, was home to 56,000 troops preparing for war.

fell ill. Forty-eight of them died. The first wave of the deadliest disease in history had begun.

FURTHER EVIDENCE

Chapter One includes information about how the influenza virus affected the troops stationed at Camp Funston in Fort Riley. What is the main point of this chapter? What key evidence supports this point? Visit the Web site below to read about the first wave of the influenza outbreak. Find a quote from the Web site that supports the main point of Chapter One.

The First Wave
www.mycorelibrary.com/flu-pandemic

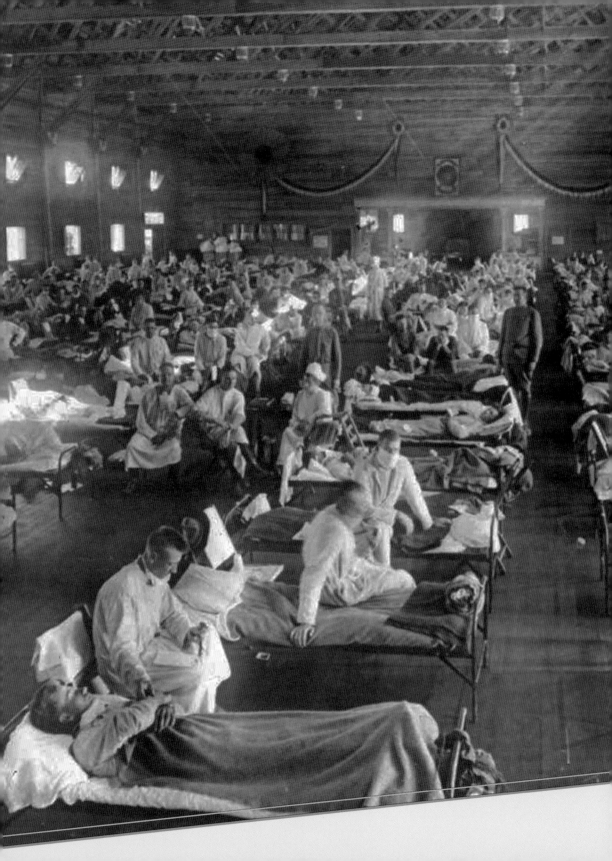

CHAPTER TWO

INFLUENZA AND THE WAR

Military officials were not very concerned about the sudden outbreak of influenza at Fort Riley. It was a time of war, and deaths at Fort Riley were not unusual. Throughout history, more soldiers have died of disease due to living in close quarters and in rough conditions than from battle wounds.

The men at Fort Riley all lived, breathed, and ate together in shared spaces. It wasn't surprising

Victims of influenza flood a hospital near Fort Riley, Kansas, in 1918.

that they all shared the same illness. History had also shown that diseases in army camps, prisons, and factories hardly ever spread to the general population. Military officials thought the flu would stay in Fort Riley. They were wrong.

The Flu Leaves Kansas

The United States entered World War I (1914–1918) in 1917. In early 1918, army bases were still training new troops for the war in Europe. As the men from Fort Riley went to other bases around the country for training, so did the flu. By September 1918, the flu was spreading so rapidly military officials had to stop drafting more soldiers. Every army camp was under quarantine to try and keep sick people

Where Did It Come From?

Researchers are still not sure how the flu began. Haskell County was a rural area, and people lived close to many farm animals. Animals can often be infected by the flu, including pigs, birds, and horses. Some researchers think the flu of 1918 started in pigs and then adapted to infect humans.

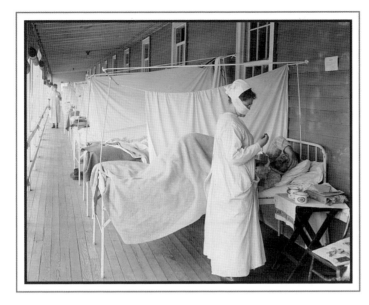

A nurse treats a flu victim at the Walter Reed Hospital Flu Ward in Washington, DC.

from infecting others. Forty percent of men in the navy had been infected, as had 36 percent of the men in the army.

Influenza Spreads to Europe

In the spring of 1918, thousands of enlisted men sailed to Europe to fight against German forces. In addition to weapons and ammunition, the men from Fort Riley brought the deadliest weapon of all: influenza. As they sailed across the Atlantic Ocean to Europe, 36 men fell ill and 6 died.

Girls in Japan wear masks to help protect themselves from the influenza outbreak.

The disease spread quickly once the troops from Fort Riley set foot on European soil. Soldiers from both sides came down with the same symptoms: high fevers and aches and pains that sometimes turned into pneumonia. By May it was clear that war plans had to change. There were not enough healthy men on either side to fight.

More Countries Fall Ill

By July influenza had spread to the European public. It also quickly made its way to other continents. Port cities around the world suffered influenza outbreaks, including cities in Africa, South America, and Asia. It is estimated that approximately 3 percent of the entire population of Africa was killed by the flu. The disease was getting stronger. And it was headed back to the United States.

The Flu Comes Home

The second wave of influenza entered the United States the same way it left: with the military. But this time, the troops returning from Europe brought back a virus that was stronger, faster, and much deadlier than the virus first seen in Haskell County. On August 28, eight men aboard a military ship in Boston, Massachusetts, were ill. Within three days, 139 more men reported symptoms. Just a few

What Is Influenza?

Influenza is a respiratory disease that spreads from person to person. The virus can leave the body through coughing and sneezing, from where it is often picked up by others' hands. Once inside the body, the virus multiplies. A virus can survive outside of the human body for only a few hours, but that is long enough to infect nearly every person it comes in contact with.

days later, in early September 1918, influenza made its way to Camp Devens.

Camp Devens

Camp Devens was an army training base 30 miles (48 km) west of Boston. It was built to hold 35,000 men. In the summer of 1918, it housed 45,000. Sleeping areas were overcrowded, so it was easy for the virus to pass from person to person.

On September 22, 1,543 soldiers reported ill to the infirmary. Numbers rose quickly. Doctors and nurses worked 16 hours a day. Even then they could not keep up with the thousands of men who needed care. The camp hospital only had room for 2,000 patients. But it held more than 8,000.

Soldiers weren't the only ones falling ill. All of the nurses and 70 of the 200 doctors also caught the virus. Dead bodies were stacked in the camp morgue. The virus left Camp Devens just as quickly as it came, leaving almost 1,000 people dead. This influenza was now a killer, claiming many lives.

A doctor stationed at Camp Devens sent a letter to a friend on September 29, 1918. In the letter, he writes about conditions at the camp. He describes cyanosis, the blue or purple discoloration of limbs from lack of oxygen, in the soldiers:

> *These men start with what appears to be an attack of. . . influenza, and when brought to the hospital they very rapidly develop the most viscous type of pneumonia that has ever been seen. Two hours after admission they have the mahogany spots over the cheekbones, and a few hours later you can begin to see the cyanosis extending from their ears and spreading all over the face. . . . It is only a matter of a few hours then until death comes, and it is simply a struggle for air until they suffocate. It is horrible.*
>
> Source: "A Letter from Camp Devens, MA." September 29, 1918. American Experience. PBS.org, 1996. Web. Accessed December 19, 2012.

Back It Up

The author of this letter is using evidence to support a point. Write a paragraph describing the point the author is making. Then write down two or three pieces of evidence the author uses to make his point.

CHAPTER THREE

THE VIRUS TAKES OVER

Camp Devens was just the beginning of the flu's reentry into the United States. Dockworkers in Boston reported fevers up to 105 degrees Fahrenheit (40°C) along with muscle and joint pain. Up to 10 percent of them developed severe pneumonia and died. Influenza continued to spread through Boston in September, killing citizens. This strain of flu was stronger and deadlier than the flu first seen in

A streetcar conductor stops a man from getting on the streetcar because he is not wearing a mask.

Haskell County back in the spring. The second wave had begun.

An Official Pandemic

Fifty thousand people in Massachusetts fell ill in September. State officials asked the United States Public Health Service (PHS) for help, but there was nobody to send. Most of the doctors and nurses had been drafted into the military in 1917. The few PHS employees who were not in the military were already taking care of flu victims or had become victims themselves.

The Great Equalizer

Whether rich or poor, young or old, an average citizen or a powerful leader, everyone had just as much chance of getting the flu as anyone else. Many leaders were infected with the disease, including US President Woodrow Wilson and future US President Franklin Roosevelt. Both men survived the flu.

Second Wave Spreads to the Public

The virus continued to spread. The very same railroads, rivers,

US President Woodrow Wilson suffered from and survived the influenza virus in 1919.

and mountain pathways that delivered people and supplies all over the country also delivered the flu. By mid-September, it appeared in California, North Dakota, Florida, Texas, and every state in between. By the first week of October, it had infected every part of the world except a few islands and Australia. Influenza was now officially a pandemic.

A Social Disease

Once the flu reached a city by rail or river, it quickly passed from person to person. While the US military fought in Europe, people at home came together for parades and fundraisers. Military victories were celebrated in the streets. Many social events were held outdoors. Hundreds, if not thousands, of people could attend. Social contact kept spirits high, but it also proved to be very dangerous.

The Killer Strain

The disease circling the globe in the fall of 1918 was very different from the spring influenza. When the virus first appeared in Haskell County, it was little more than a three-day fever.

Other Deadly Diseases

Influenza was not the only disease taking lives in the early 1900s. Other deadly diseases included cholera, tuberculosis, and the bubonic plague. Cholera and tuberculosis were caused by bacteria found in unclean drinking water. The plague was a virus carried by rats and passed through the air between humans.

22

A crowd gathers outside of a church in Fresno, California, to pray for an end to the flu virus.

Now the symptoms were more severe. The death toll exploded.

Most people who caught the virus survived, but those who didn't suffered greatly. Some died within hours of showing their first symptoms. Their lungs filled with fluid, preventing oxygen from getting to the rest of the body. Death was not far behind.

An Alarming Death Rate

Everyone was at risk. While other strains of the flu attacked the very young and the very old, this flu was extremely dangerous for young adults. Between 8 and 10 percent of all people in their 20s and 30s were killed by the virus. Overall, 675,000 Americans died from influenza in 1918 and 1919. Half of those deaths occurred between September and December 1918.

Communities Shut Down

Many people were either too sick to work or too afraid of catching the disease. Businesses shut down. Garbage piled up in the streets. The only businesses that thrived were the funeral parlors, and they had more work than they could handle. Most funeral parlors ran out of caskets immediately. Some undertakers took advantage of grieving families and raised the prices for funerals. Cemeteries charged burial fees, but there were so many deaths that family members often had to dig the graves themselves.

Children of families sick with influenza stand in line to receive food from volunteers.

25

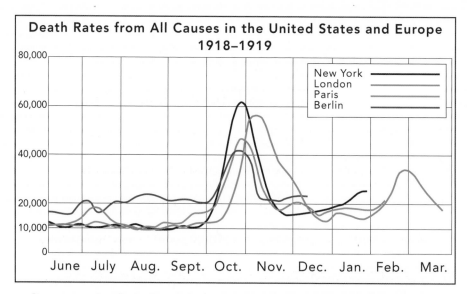

Death Rates from All Causes in the United States and Europe 1918–1919

New York
London
Paris
Berlin

June July Aug. Sept. Oct. Nov. Dec. Jan. Feb. Mar.

Influenza Spikes Overall Death Rates in the United States and Europe

This chart shows total death rates from all causes in New York, London, Paris, and Berlin in 1918 and 1919. Notice how the death rate increased dramatically in October and November as the flu virus spread. How does this chart help you understand how deadly the virus was and how it affected so many people? Is there anything you are surprised to see? Explain your answer.

When the funeral parlors ran out of caskets, bodies were left in hospital morgues. Victims who died at home often stayed there until family members could figure out what to do. They were put in a corner and then wrapped in sheets or covered in ice. Others were left on the bed where they died.

Those Left Behind

Millions of people survived the flu. Many of them faced nearly unlivable conditions. Entire families became ill at once. Many children were orphaned after their parents passed away. Others watched their brothers and sisters die. Hospitals were overflowing with patients, and many sick people were turned away. Community centers and schools became emergency hospitals run by medical and nursing students.

Influenza stayed in a community for just a few weeks, but the effects would last for years. People wondered why the disease kept spreading. They wanted to know when there would be a cure.

CHAPTER FOUR

TREATMENT AND PREVENTION

Medical care in 1918 was much less advanced than it is today. One in five US children died before the age of five because of infectious diseases. The average life span in the early 1900s was only 53 years for men and 54 years for women. Change was happening in the field of medicine but not fast enough. When the influenza virus appeared

Citizens, including policemen, in many cities were required to wear masks during the pandemic.

The Spanish Flu

The strain of flu that caused the pandemic of 1918 was also called the Spanish flu. Spain, like many European countries, was hit hard by influenza in May and June 1918. Spain was the only country that reported how bad the flu was in newspapers. Stories of this "Spanish flu" were picked up worldwide, which made it seem like the disease started there.

in 1918, doctors had no idea what they were dealing with.

The Search for a Cure

Doctors and scientists did not know much about viruses, but they did know about bacteria. Some believed bacteria caused the flu virus. They found bacteria when they examined the dead bodies. But they couldn't seem to link bacteria with the virus.

Researchers tried to prevent the illness. By 1918 vaccines prevented many illnesses. Some in the medical field decided to create their own vaccines made from the blood and mucus of flu victims. The vaccines did not work.

This street cleaner in New York wears a mask while he works.

Treatment Attempts

While researchers tried to find a cure, public health officials tried to stop the virus from spreading. Some techniques they used, such as washing hands before meals and sterilizing eating and drinking utensils, are still used today.

Other techniques were not as effective. Nobody knew what was causing the flu, so it was hard to know how to prevent it. Many cities required people to wear gauze masks in public. Others banned spitting. These methods helped, but they weren't enough to stop the pandemic.

Rumors Run Wild

Posters about how to prevent the disease were put up all across the country. But they were only somewhat effective. Most of the information about the flu spread by word of mouth, and very little of it was correct. This was especially true when it came to the origin of the flu and its treatment.

Many people thought the disease was a crime of war. They thought German spies brought influenza germs across the Atlantic Ocean and released them into Boston Harbor. Others thought influenza was caused by things such as coal dust, fleas, or dirty dishwater.

This public health warning urges people to leave their windows open for fresh air.

Those infected with the virus went to great lengths to get rid of it. Home remedies were popular, as were fake medicines that did nothing but empty people's pocketbooks. Some doctors wrapped people in blankets to make them sweat.

The Disease Disappears

Since there was no cure in sight, the ill were quarantined in their homes. Schools, theaters, pool halls, and churches often closed. These efforts slowed the spread of the virus. By November 1918, fewer new cases of the flu were reported. By the summer of 1919, it had disappeared completely.

Home Remedies

Folk remedies were popular during the influenza pandemic. Some mothers made children stuff salt up their noses. Others used onions. One mother in Pennsylvania fed her children everything from onion omelets to onion salads to onion soup at every meal. None of her eight children got sick.

The following is an excerpt from a navy publication that taught sailors how to prevent the spread of influenza. It was published on September 26, 1918:

> Influenza is caused by a germ. . .which lives but a short time outside of the body. Fresh air and sunshine kill the germ in a few minutes.
>
> The disease is spread by the moist secretions from the nose and throats of infected persons.
>
> Protect yourself from infection, keep well, and do not get hysterical over the epidemic.
>
> Avoid being sprayed by the nose and throat secretions of others.
>
> Beware of those who are coughing and sneezing. . . .
>
> Secure at least seven hours sleep. Avoid physical fatigue.
>
> Do not sleep or sit around in damp clothing.
>
> Keep the feet dry.

Source: Naval Districts and Shore Establishments, Division of Sanitation. "No. 130212-0: Influenza." Circular No. 1. Washington, DC: Department of the Army, September 26, 1918. Print.

Changing Minds

Imagine how people who hadn't received this information reacted to the flu. Where might they think it had come from?

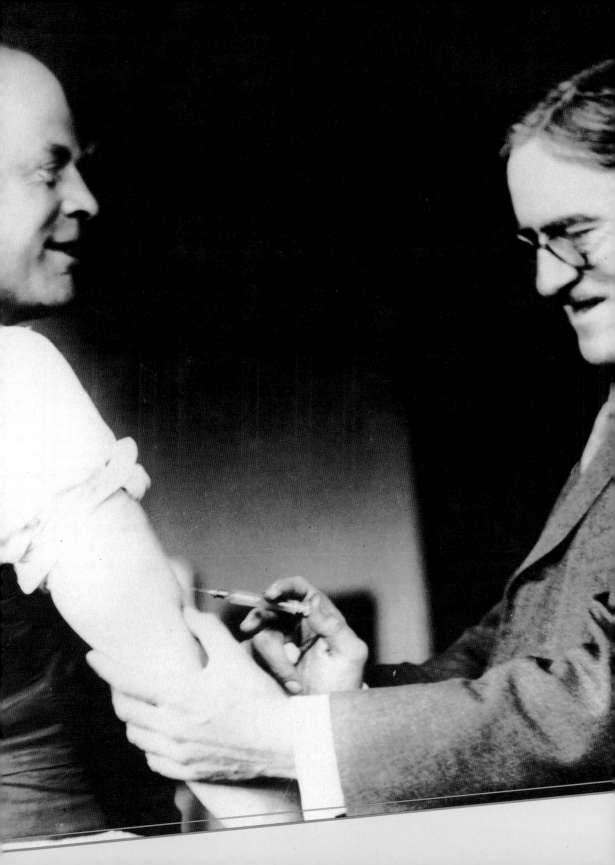

HOW INFLUENZA CHANGED THE UNITED STATES

The influenza virus of 1918 killed approximately 25 out of every 1,000 people infected. The disease was devastating, and the effects lasted for years. The memory of the influenza pandemic was a painful one. Those who survived didn't talk about it much.

Nobody knows exactly how many people died from the flu. Unlike today, there were no tests to see

A doctor injects a Boston man in hopes of fighting off influenza.

if a person actually had the disease. People were infected so quickly that states couldn't keep records of all illnesses and deaths. Some countries in Asia and Africa didn't keep records at all.

The Lasting Effects of Disease

Today it is estimated that 30 to 50 million people worldwide were killed by the flu pandemic of 1918. It was the cause of more deaths than any illness in history.

Flu Epidemics in History

The earliest known widespread outbreak of influenza was in 412 BCE in Greece. It showed up again in Ancient Rome and then later in England during the Middle Ages. It was not common practice to keep records of disease until the late 1700s.

The United States Deals with Disease

The impact on the US population was staggering. The average life expectancy dropped by 12 years between 1917 and 1918. Families lost loved ones. Some children

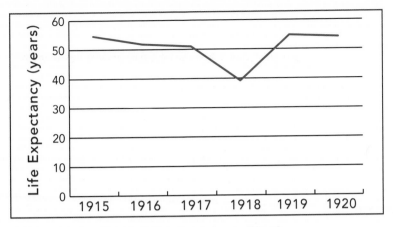

US Estimated Life Expectancy at Birth
This graph shows the average expected life span of people born in the United States between 1915 and 1920. What does the graph tell you about the average life span during that time? Based on this graph, how did the influenza outbreak of 1918 affect the average life expectancy? What else can you learn from the graph?

lost one or both parents. Nearly 10 percent of young adults died.

The economy also suffered. Businesses shut their doors during the outbreak to stop the spread of disease. Many never reopened because of death or money loss from shutting down during the pandemic.

Searching for Answers

After the pandemic ended in 1919, scientists continued to study influenza. The first breakthrough came in 1933. During a mild flu outbreak in London, researchers discovered that influenza was a virus. Vaccines can prevent viruses. The first flu vaccine was created in 1944.

The process for controlling future outbreaks was ready by the 1950s. Researchers continued studying the disease. They learned that the flu virus starts in birds, which then infect other animals, such as pigs. It then changes to adapt to humans.

Influenza is still a concern today. But the 1918 pandemic pushed doctors and scientists to find out exactly what causes it, how it spreads, and how it can be prevented. Today's vaccines are a tribute to the many lives lost during the most deadly outbreak in world history.

How Do Vaccines Work?

Vaccines are a weakened form of a disease that is injected into the body. It is not enough to make someone sick, but it forces the body to make antibodies to fight off the disease. Those antibodies will protect the body if it is exposed to the actual disease.

This granite headstone stands in a group of other headstones bearing the names and dates of young men who died from the 1918 influenza pandemic.

EXPLORE ONLINE

Chapter Five focuses on how the influenza pandemic of 1918 affected the United States and the rest of the world. The Web site below focuses on the effects of the pandemic. How is the information given in the Web site different from the information in this chapter? What information is the same? How do the two sources present the information differently? What can you learn from this Web site?

The Legacy of the Pandemic
www.mycorelibrary.com/flu-pandemic

IMPORTANT DATES

Feb. 1918

A mysterious disease appears in Haskell County, Kansas. It causes high fevers, body aches, and often leads to pneumonia. Several people die.

Feb. 1918

Between February 28 and March 2, three men from Haskell County arrive at Camp Funston in Fort Riley, Kansas, spreading influenza.

Mar. 1918

The first case of influenza is reported at Camp Funston in Fort Riley, Kansas, on March 11.

Aug. 1918

Sailors aboard a ship in Boston, Massachusetts, come down with the flu in late August. Within days, it reaches citizens and begins the pandemic's second wave.

Sept. 1918

Military officials stop drafting soldiers due to influenza. Every army camp is under quarantine.

Sept. 1918

1,543 soldiers report ill to the Camp Devens infirmary on September 22.

May 1918

Influenza appears in Europe, infecting troops on both sides of World War I.

July 1918

Influenza spreads to citizens in Europe.

Oct. 1918

Influenza has reached every part of the world with the exception of Australia and a few remote islands.

1919

The influenza pandemic is officially over by summer.

1944

The first flu vaccine is created.

STOP AND THINK

Say What?

Learning about diseases can mean learning a lot of new vocabulary. Find five words in this book you have never seen or heard before. Use a dictionary to find out what they mean. Then write the meanings in your own words and use each word in a sentence.

You Are There

Chapter Two includes information about the influenza outbreak at Camp Devens in Massachusetts. The hospital had thousands more cases of influenza than it could handle. Imagine you are a doctor or nurse working in the infirmary. Your coworkers are falling ill, and you are running out of supplies. How do you respond? Explain what you see, hear, and feel.

Take a Stand

Chapter Three mentions that some funeral-home owners raised their prices during the pandemic. Do you think this was a good business decision or an unfair practice? Write a short essay explaining your opinion. Make sure to give reasons for your opinion and facts and details to support those reasons.

Surprise Me

Chapter Five discusses the lasting effects of the influenza pandemic in the United States. After reading this book, what two or three facts did you find most surprising? Write a few sentences about each fact. Why did you find them surprising?

GLOSSARY

cyanosis
a condition in which the skin turns blue or purple from lack of oxygen

infectious
capable of being passed to someone else by germs that enter the body

infirmary
a place where sick people stay and are cared for

morgue
a place where the bodies of dead people are kept until they are buried or cremated

pandemic
an occurrence in which a disease spreads very quickly and affects a large number of people over a wide area or throughout the world

pneumonia
a serious disease that affects the lungs and makes it difficult to breathe

quarantine
to keep a person away from others to prevent a disease from spreading

quarters
the place where someone lives

suffocate
to die because you are unable to breathe

vaccine
a substance made of dead, weak, or living organisms that a human can take to help fight the disease caused by the organisms

LEARN MORE

Books

Barnard, Bryn. *Outbreak: Plagues that Changed History.* New York: Crown Publishers, 2005.

Kent, Susan Kingsley. *The Influenza Pandemic of 1918–1919.* Boston: Bedford/St. Martin's, 2013.

Peters, Stephanie True. *The 1918 Influenza Pandemic.* New York: Benchmark Books, 2005.

Web Links

To learn more about the flu pandemic of 1918, visit ABDO Publishing Company online at **www.abdopublishing.com**. Web sites about the flu pandemic of 1918 are featured on our Book Links page. These links are routinely monitored and updated to provide the most current information available.

Visit **www.mycorelibrary.com** for free additional tools for teachers and students.

INDEX

ABOUT THE AUTHOR

Kristin Marciniak lives in Kansas City, Missouri, with her husband, son, and golden retriever. She spends her free time quilting, knitting, reading, and chasing after her very energetic toddler.